EDGAR H. ADAMS'

Plates

of

LYMAN H. LOW'S

Hard Times Tokens

Quarterman Publications, Inc.
Lawrence, Massachusetts

This work is a lithographic compilation of Edgar H. Adams' set of 15 individual photographic plates of Lyman Haynes Low's Hard Times Tokens originally produced circa 1914. Certain individual token illustrations on these plates have been photochemically enhanced in this edition. Alfred Z. Reed's introduction to the Hard Times Token section of the 1942 edition of *The Standard Catalogue of United States Coins and Tokens From 1652 to Present Day* has been reprinted as an introduction. William Forrester Dunham's *Instant Finding List* of 1910 has additionally been reprinted in a form adapted from publication in Volume 37 of *The Numismatist*, modified to include Adams' plate numbers and other minor alterations.

International Standard Book Number: 0-88000-120-8
Printed in the United States of America

Quarterman Publications, Inc.
5 South Union Street, Lawrence, Massachusetts 01843

HARD TIMES TOKENS 1832-1844

Lyman H. Low's famous list of one hundred and eighty-three Hard Times Tokens is a selection from among a much larger number of private issues put forth during a stirring period of twelve years. President Andrew Jackson disapproved of a fiscal system under which public funds were deposited in a single privately controlled institution, the Bank of the United States. On July 10, 1832, accepting the challenge of Henry Clay and the financial interests of the country, he vetoed a bill to continue the Bank in existence after the expiration of its charter in 1836. This action transformed the personal animosities of rival politicians into a sustained popular controversy over fundamental political principles. The already dominant Republican party of Thomas Jefferson split into two violently opposed groups. On the one side Clay's supporters, reinforced by former Federalists, fought vigorously to restore the Bank. After their failure, as "National-Republicans," to defeat Jackson for reelection in 1832, they broadened their ranks to include all who attacked his methods as dictatorial and unconstitutional, and campaigned under the name of "Whigs." On the other side the "Democratic-Republican" or, more briefly, the "Democratic" party of Jackson and of his successor Martin Van Buren not only succeeded in warding off these attacks but inaugurated supplementary reforms. They ceased to deposit governmental receipts in the central Bank while it was still alive. After state banks had shown themselves to be unsafe depositaries, they established the independent sub-treasury system. They were responsible also for changing the coinage ratio of gold and silver so as to bring gold coins for the first time into circulation, and they refused to accept anything except metallic currency in payment for public lands. Van Buren's defeat for reelection by the Whig candidate, William H. Harrison, in 1840, proved to be only a temporary setback to the financial policy of the Democrats, who returned to power in 1844. The period ends with the emergence, that year, of new political issues, notably that of the annexation of Texas, foreshadowing war with Mexico and a reopening of the slavery controversy.

Two causes were responsible for the large number of private issues in copper, brass and white metal during this period. In the first place, the suffrage had recently been broadened and there was a general shift from the choice of presidential electors by legislatures to our present system of direct vote by the people. This change in political methods stimulated a corresponding popularization of one of the two main branches of numismatics, medals as distinguished from coins. Cheap and crudely executed campaign pieces, the forerunners of our present campaign buttons and pins, appeared possibly as early as 1824 and certainly by 1828, but in no great number until 1834. They were then first struck, with improved workmanship, on flans of approximately the size of the official large cent.

A second powerful stimulus to the production of tokens was provided by the economic depression to which the period owes its name. Times were intermittently "hard" from the winter of 1833-34 until 1842, being at their worst during the twelve months following May 10, 1837, when all the banks in the country were unable to meet their obligations. Jackson's radical reforms were unsettling in themselves, and their effects were deliberately aggravated by the Bank of the United States in the hope of either frightening or overturning the administration. Credit, moreover, had been greatly overextended, both at home and abroad, and a severe reaction was in any event due. The attendant discrediting of large banknotes and hoarding of gold left, as the only medium available for current cash payments, subsidiary silver, or, when this also was hoarded, "shinplasters" for small amounts, issued by municipalities, individuals or banks. This, in turn, made it necessary to use copper pieces for small payments formerly made in silver. There was also a great increase in the number of articles, such as penny newspapers, which were priced at less than the silver half dime. The result was to create a demand for copper money, which the official coinage was unable to meet. Private enterprise rose to the emergency by issuing pieces of the size, and usually in the metal, of the contemporary large cent.

The tokens selected by Low for his list were usually, although not always, of this size. In addition to many Merchants' Tokens, he included some fifty which carried political propaganda, and about half that number of pieces which were issued only as a circulating medium and did not advertise at the same time either a business firm or product, or a political candidate, party or cause.

INDEX TO LOW AND ADAMS PLATE NUMBERS

22 — Female head. 9 berries outside, 6 inside. 15 stars. *PLATE II, PLATE X*
23 — Female head. 9 berries outside, 4 inside. *PLATE II*
24 — Female Head. 6 berries outside, 6 inside. Bushnell strike. *PLATE XII*
25 — Female Head. 7 berries outside, 8 inside. Small date. Plain hair cord. Bushnell. *PLATE XIII*
26 — Female Head. 7 berries outside, 8 inside. Large date. Beaded hair cord. Bushnell. *PLATE XII*
27 — Female Head. 7 berries outside, 8 inside. Scroll around motto. Bushnell. *PLATE XII*
28 — Female head. 6 berries outside, 7 inside. *PLATE II*
170 — Female Head. Obverse of No. 28. Reverse, 5 berries inside, 5 outside.
29 — Female head. 4 berries outside, 4 inside. *PLATE II*
30 — Female head. 4 berries outside, 6 inside. *PLATE II*
31 — Female head. 4 berries outside, 6 inside. Scroll ends under second U of UNUM. Curl right. *PLATE II*
32 — Female head. 4 berries outside, 6 inside. Scroll ends under N of UNUM. Curl left. *PLATE II*
33 — Female Head of No. 32. 3 berries outside, 5 inside. Scroll ends under N of UNUM. *PLATE II*
34 — Female Head. 4 berries outside, 6 inside. Scroll ends under second U of UNUM. Curl left. (Heads of Nos. 34 to 40 are the same.) *PLATE II*
35 — Female head. 3 berries outside, 6 inside. Rev. die of No. 31 retouched, berries enlarged. Berry on leaf pointing to C in DEFENCE and that pointing to N in NOT are cut out. *PLATE X*
36 — Female head. 2 berries outside, 6 inside. *PLATE III*
37 — Female head. MINT DROP. 3 berries outside, 6 inside. *PLATE III*
38 — Female head. MINT DROP. 3 berries outside, 6 inside. *PLATE III*
39 — Female head. NOT ONE CENT. 27 stars. *PLATE III*
40 — Female head. MAY TENTH 1837. Leaves. *PLATE III*
67 — Female head. 1841. MAY TENTH. Leaves. *PLATE V*
68 — Female head. 3 berries outside, 6 inside. Obv., 5 roses left, 4 roses right. *PLATE V*
69 — Female head. 3 berries outside, 5 inside. *PLATE V*
70 — Female head. 3 berries outside, 4 inside. Bushnell strike. *PLATE XI*
71 — Female head. 3 berries outside, 5 inside. Scroll ends under N of UNUM. Obv., roses. Bushnell strike. *PLATE XII*
55 — Female head. LOCO FOCO. MINT DROP. *PLATE IV*
150 — Gibbs, J. *PLATE XI, PLATE XIII*
151 — Gibbs, W. *PLATE IX*
7 — Glorious Whig Victory. Liberty cap. *PLATE I*
175 — Gustin & Blake. *PLATE XIV*
176 — Gustin & Blake. *PLATE XIV*
85 — Hall, J. Walker & Walton. *PLATE XIV*
49 — Half Cent Worth of Pure Copper. *PLATE III*
78 — Handy, W. A. *PLATE V*
131 — Haselton & Palmer. A. C. Smith. *PLATE VIII*
79 — Haskins, W. P. Rev., Lafayette. *PLATE V*
80 — Haskins, W. P. Rev., Woodworth's Patent. *PLATE V*
74 — Hathaway, Ephraim A. *PLATE V*
173 — Herring, H.
81 — Howell Works Garden. Grapes. *PLATE V*
163 — Howell Works Garden. Rose. *PLATE XI*
102 — Huckel, Burrows & Jennings. Brass. *PLATE XIII*
177 — Huckel, Burrows & Jennings. Brass, silvered before striking. *PLATE XIV*
178 — Huckel, Burrows & Jennings. White Metal. *PLATE XIII*
122 — Jarvis, George A. Stars. Obverse of No. 32. *PLATE VII*
123 — Jarvis, George A. Leaves. Obverse of No. 30. *PLATE VII*

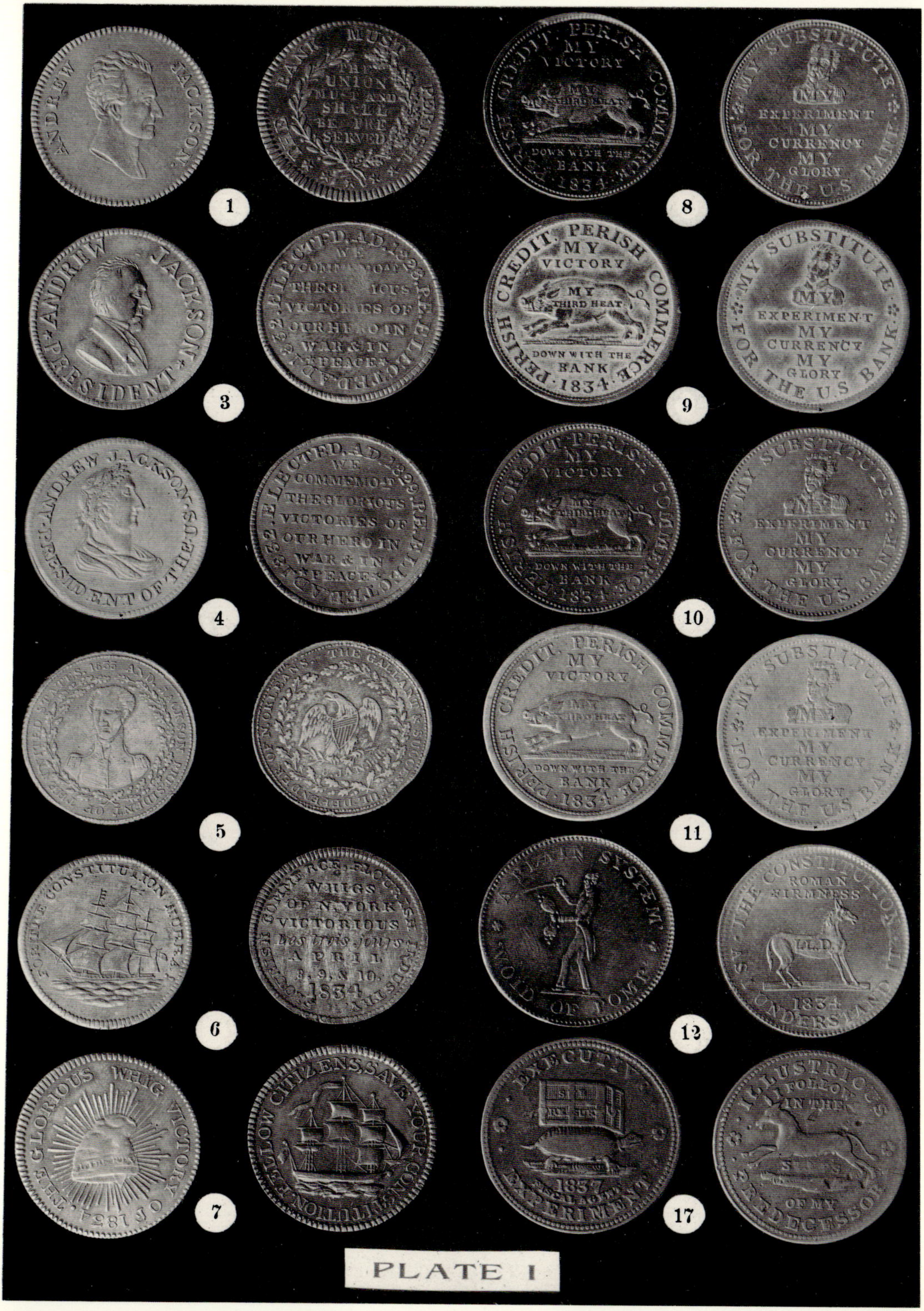
ANDREW JACKSON.
1
MY VICTORY
DOWN WITH THE BANK 1834
8
MY SUBSTITUTE FOR THE U.S. BANK
MY EXPERIMENT MY CURRENCY MY GLORY
ANDREW JACKSON PRESIDENT
3
PERISH CREDIT. PERISH COMMERCE.
MY THIRD HEAT
9
ELECTED A.D. 1828
WE COMMEMORATE THE GLORIOUS VICTORIES OF OUR HERO IN WAR & IN PEACE
4
10
5
11
WHIGS OF N. YORK VICTORIOUS
APRIL 8. 9. & 10. 1834
6
ROMAN FIRMNESS
L.L.D.
1834
12
THE GLORIOUS WHIG VICTORY OF 1834
FELLOW CITIZENS, SAVE YOUR CONSTITUTION
7
1837
17
IN THE
OF MY
PLATE I

PLATE II

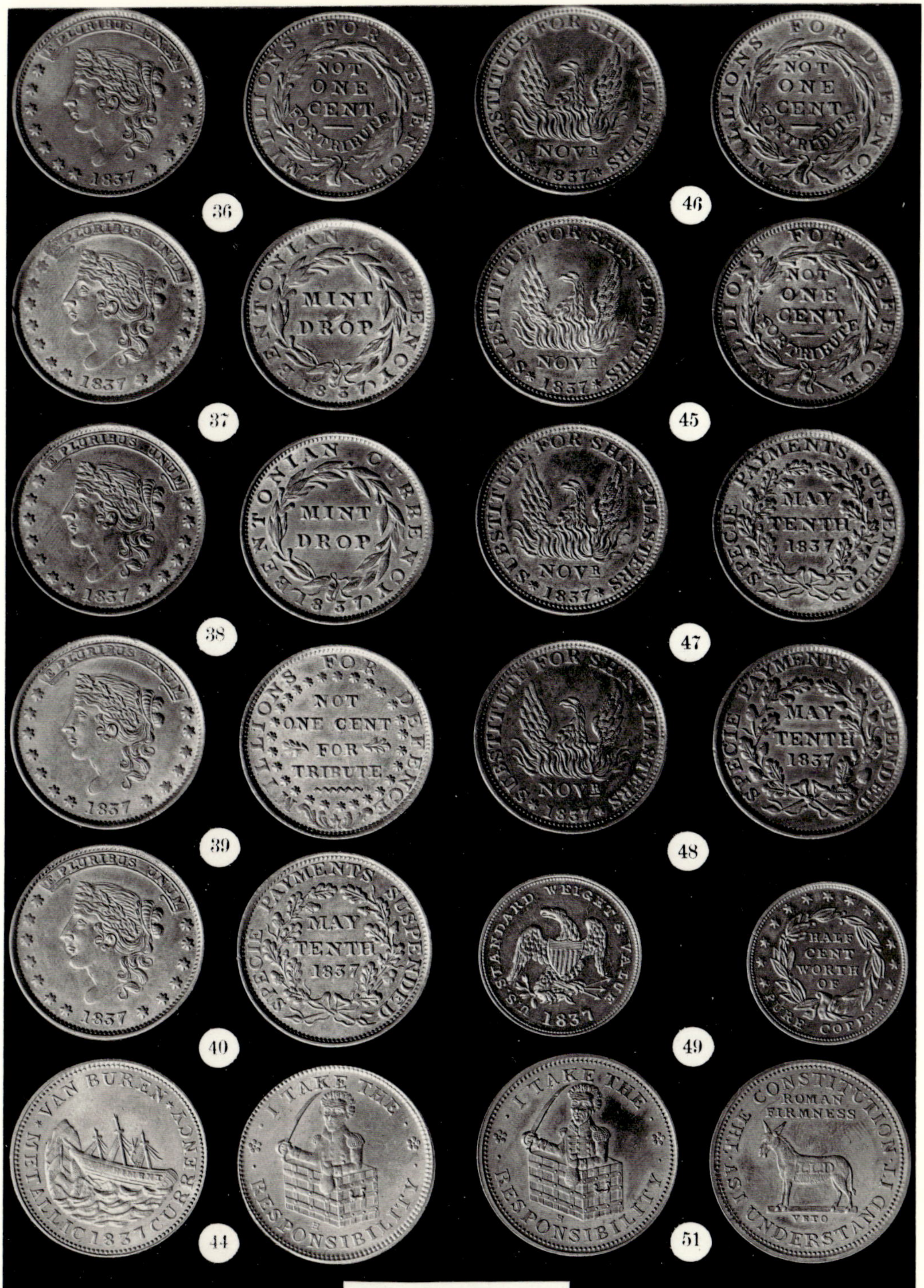
E PLURIBUS UNUM
1837
MILLIONS FOR DEFENCE
NOT ONE CENT FOR TRIBUTE
SUBSTITUTE FOR SHIN PLASTERS
NOVR 1837
36
46
ENTONIAN CURRENCY
MINT DROP
1837
37
45
38
SPECIE PAYMENTS SUSPENDED
MAY TENTH 1837
47
39
48
40
U.S. STANDARD WEIGHT & VALUE
HALF CENT WORTH OF PURE COPPER
49
VAN BUREN METALLIC CURRENCY 1837
I TAKE THE RESPONSIBILITY
THE CONSTITUTION AS I UNDERSTAND IT
ROMAN FIRMNESS
LLD
VETO
44
51

PLATE III

PLATE IV

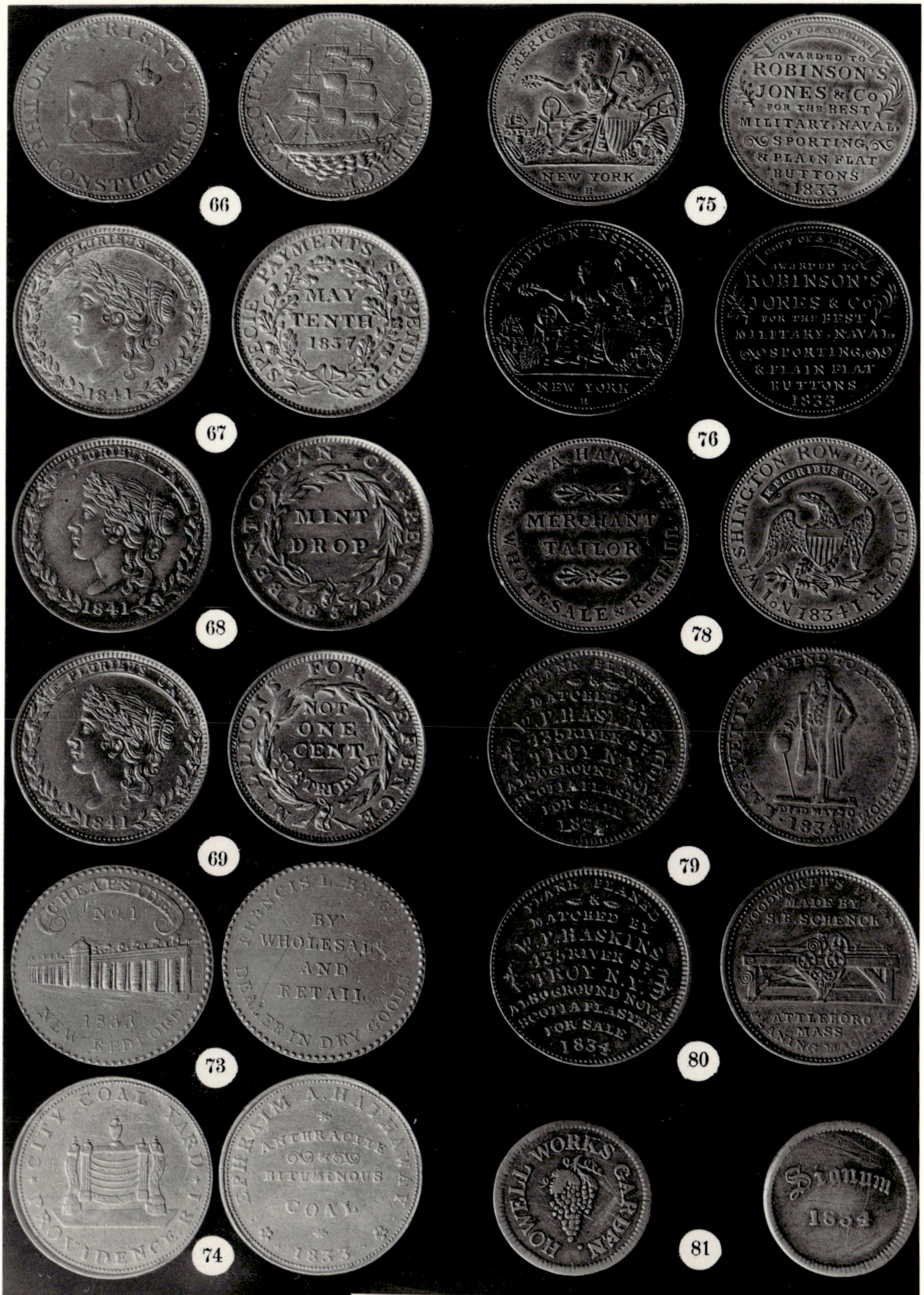

PLATE V

84
96
86
97
92
98
93
99
94
100
95
101
MADE BY
S.B.SCHENCK
ATTLEBORO
MASS.
GROOVING,
OR JOINTING,
18 FEET OF BOARDS
OR PLANK IN A
MINUTE
1834
BUILT 1827
BURNT 1835
NOT
ONE
CENT
FOR TRIBUTE
MILLIONS FOR DEFENCE
BOOTS, SHOES
HATS, CAPS, FURS
LOWELL
DIED MAY 20
BUCKLIN'S BOOK KEEPING
TROY
1835
MERCHANT'S
EXCHANGE
NEW YORK JOINT STOCK EXCHANGE COMPANY
No 8
TONTINE
BUILDING
WALL
STt
WALSH'S
GENERAL STORE
LANSINGBURGH
(N.Y)
1835
SPEED THE PLOUGH
IT FEEDS ALL
JEWELERS
&
WATCHMAKERS
NOs 25 & 27
CHEAPSIDE
PROVIDENCE
R.I
1835
LAFAYETTE A FRIEND TO AMERICA & FREEDOM
DIED MAY 20
1834
LANSINBURG
NEW-YORK

PLATE VI

PLATE VII

NATH. MARCH BOOKSELLER & STATIONER No. 7 EXCHANGE BUILDINGS PORTSMOUTH N.H 1837
WILLIAM SIMES & CO DEALERS IN TEAS, WINES, & GROCERIES No. 1 PEIRCE'S BUILDINGS PORTSMOUTH N.H
124
E. F. SISE & CO GENERAL COMMISSION AND FORWARDING MERCHANTS PORTSMOUTH N.H.
IMPORTERS OF CROCKERY AND GLASS WARE DEALERS IN COAL 1837
132
E PLURIBUS UNUM 1837
S. MAYCOCK & CO. EVERPOINTED PENCIL CASE MANUFACTURERS SAML. MAYCOCK JOHN HAGUE CITY HALL PLACE
125
TIME IS MONEY
SMITHS CLOCK ESTABLISHMENT No 7½ BOWERY NEW YORK 1837
133
1837
S. MAYCOCK & CO. EVERPOINTED PENCIL CASE MANUFACTURERS SAML. MAYCOCK JOHN HAGUE CITY HALL PLACE
126
TIME IS MONEY
SMITHS CLOCK ESTABLISHMENT No 7½ BOWERY NEW YORK 1837
134
PHALONS NEW & SPLENDID STYLE OF HAIR CUTTING
No 35 BOWERY 1837 NEW YORK
127
TIME IS MONEY
SMITHS CLOCK ESTABLISHMENT No 7½ BOWERY NEW YORK 1837
135
J. M. L. & W. H. SCOVILL 1837 WATERBURY CON.
GILT BUTTONS OF EVERY DESCRIPTION SHEET BRASS PLATED METAL & GOLD PLATE
130
TIME IS MONEY
SMITHS CLOCK ESTABLISHMENT No 7½ BOWERY NEW YORK 1837
136
A. C. SMITH DEALER IN CROCKERY, GLASS, CHINA & BRITANNIA WARE, LOOKING GLASSES &c. DOVER, N.H. 1837
HASELTON & PALMER DEALERS IN DRY-GOODS, GROCERIES & STRAW-BONNETS No. 2 COCHECO BLOCK DOVER, N.H.
131
TIME IS MONEY
138
SMITHS CLOCK ESTABLISHMENT No 7½ BOWERY NEW YORK 1837

PLATE VIII

PLATE IX

PLATE X

PLATE XI

24
NOT ONE CENT FOR TRIBUTE
120
1837
FEUCHTWANGER'S ONE CENT COMPOSITION
E PLURIBUS UNUM 1837
MILLIONS FOR DEFENCE NOT ONE CENT FOR TRIBUTE
26
E. F. RUSSELL I-O-U $12\frac{1}{2}$c
1837
128
E PLURIBUS UNUM 1837
MILLIONS FOR DEFENCE NOT ONE CENT FOR TRIBUTE
27
156
MARTIN VAN BUREN THE PEOPLES CHOICE
SUB TREASURY & DEMOCRACY
57
M. VAN BUREN
INDEPENDENT TREASURY JULY 4, 1840
162
E PLURIBUS UNUM 1841
MILLIONS FOR DEFENCE NOT ONE CENT FOR TRIBUTE
71
I TAKE THE RESPONSIBILITY
THE CONSTITUTION AS I UNDERSTAND IT
ROMAN FIRMNESS
LL.D
VETO
171
SHOWS AT ONE VIEW THE EXACT STATE OF YOUR BUSINESS SECOND EDITION IMPROVED, PRICE ONE DOLLAR
SHOWS THE INTEREST AT A GLANCE OF ANY SUM FOR ANY TIME AT 6 AND 7 PER CENT PRICE FROM 25 CENTS TO 2 DOLLARS
77
G W B 18 43
181

PLATE XII

5
87
BAKERS &
CONFECTIONERS.
NOT
ONE
CENT
1837
21
89
NOT
ONE
CENT
FOR TRIBUTE
25
DEALERS
IN
GROCERIES
CHOICE WINES
1836
178
BOAT STORES
AND
SHIP CHANDLERY
MAIN STREET
St. LOUIS
CHEAPSIDE
No. 1
1833
NEW BEDFORD
FRANCIS L. BRIGHAM
BY
WHOLESALE
AND
RETAIL.
DEALER IN DRY GOODS
72
BURROWS & JENNINGS
DEALERS
IN
GROCERIES
CHOICE WINES
&c &c.
1836
102
BOAT STORES.
AND
SHIP CHANDLERY
MAIN STREET
St. LOUIS
SHOWS AT
ONE VIEW, THE
EXACT STATE OF
YOUR BUSINESS.
SECOND EDITION
IMPROVED, PRICE
ONE DOLLAR.
TROY, N.Y.
SHOWS THE
INTEREST AT A
GLANCE, OF ANY SUM
FOR ANY TIME.
AT 6 AND 7 PER CENT
PRICE
FROM 25 CENTS TO
2 DOLLARS.
TROY, N.Y.
77
150
OF
MEDALS
AND
TOKENS
&c
NEW ORLEANS
1834
IMPORTERS
OF
HARDWARES
GUNS & PISTOLS
CUTLERY &c
82
OHIO
158
NO. 34
MERWIN ST
1843

PLATE XIII